STEM *trailblazer* BIOS

NINTENDO VIDEO GAME DESIGNER
SHIGERU MIYAMOTO

KARI CORNELL

Lerner Publications
Minneapolis

For Brian, Will, and Theo, who love to play and create

Lerner Publications Company
A division of Lerner Publishing Group, Inc.
241 First Avenue North
Minneapolis, MN 55401 USA

For reading levels and more information, look up this title at www.lernerbooks.com.

Content Consultant: Jonathan Ferguson, Instructor, Game Design and Production in The Game Studio at Champlain College

Library of Congress Cataloging-in-Publication Data

Cornell, Kari.
    Nintendo video game designer Shigeru Miyamoto / Kari Cornell.
        pages   cm. — (STEM trailblazer bios)
    Includes index.
    Audience: Age: 7–11.
    Audience: Grades: 4 to 6.
    ISBN 978-1-4677-9531-9 (lb : alk. paper) — ISBN 978-1-4677-9723-8 (pb : alk. paper) — ISBN 978-1-4677-9724-5 (eb pdf)
    1. Miyamoto, Shigeru, 1952– —Juvenile literature. 2. Nintendo Kabushiki Kaisha—Biography—Juvenile literature. 3. Nintendo video games—Design—History—Juvenile literature. I. Title.
GV1469.32.C67 2016
794.8—dc23   2015017900

Manufactured in the United States of America
1 – BP – 12/31/15

The images in this book are used with the permission of: © JTB MEDIA CREATION, Inc./Alamy, p. 4; FELIX ORDONEZ/REUTERS//Newscom, p. 5; © Patrick Batchelder/Alamy, p. 7; Courtesy YouTube, p. 9; © The Asahi Shimbun/Getty Images, p. 10; via http://nintendo.wikia.com/, p. 12; © ZUMA Press, Inc./Alamy, p. 14; © Jamaway/Alamy, pp. 16, 22, 23; © ArcadeImages/Alamy, pp. 17, 19; © iStockphoto.com/robtek, p. 20; © Yvonne Hemsey/Getty Images, p. 24; © Guy Bell/Alamy, p. 26; © T.M.O.Pictures/Alamy, p. 27; © Ralf-Finn Hestoft/Corbis, p. 28.

Front cover: Michael Bowles/ZUMApress/Newscom; © iStockphoto.com/ilbusca (background).

Main body text set in Adrianna Regular 13/22. Typeface provided by Chank.

CONTENTS

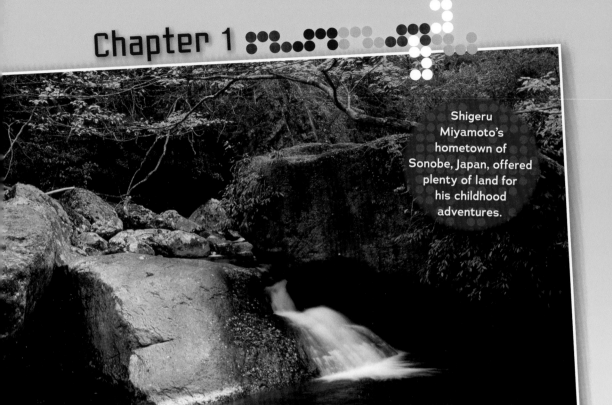

Shigeru Miyamoto's hometown of Sonobe, Japan, offered plenty of land for his childhood adventures.

A NATURAL EXPLORER

The woods around eight-year-old Shigeru Miyamoto's home in Sonobe, Japan, were the perfect playground. Shigeru spent hours climbing trees, exploring, and fishing in a nearby stream. Once he discovered a narrow hole in the

ground. He had no idea where the hole would lead, but he wanted to find out.

The next day, he came back with a lantern and wiggled his way through the dark tunnel to a cave underground. Shigeru loved exploring the cave. He liked the scary but exciting feeling of not knowing what was around the next corner. Shigeru didn't know it then, but these childhood adventures would inspire the video games he would create years later.

Although he is best known for his game ideas, Miyamoto is also a talented artist.

EARLY YEARS

Shigeru Miyamoto was born in Sonobe, Japan, on November 16, 1952. He lived with his father and mother in a home that had been in the family for generations. When Shigeru was a child, the family didn't own a television or a car, so Shigeru rarely watched television shows or went to the movies. But a few times a year, the family would take the train to the nearby city of Kyoto for a special outing to a movie theater. Shigeru often saw animated films, movies brought to life by artists and designers. Shigeru loved feeling swept up in an exciting story.

At home, Shigeru enjoyed listening to stories. But he did more than listen. He told stories too. He drew pictures and made cartoon flip-books. After school, he drew cartoons with

TECH TALK

"I know as a child, I was really interested in becoming a manga artist, to create my own stories and illustrate them and present something that people would be interested in reading and looking at as well."
—Shigeru Miyamoto

Manga was a big influence on Miyamoto and his artistic style.

other members of a cartoon club he started. Once each year, members of the club displayed their work at a cartoon exhibit. He also gave puppet shows using puppets he made out of sticks and string. As Shigeru grew older, he began to carve wooden puppets using his grandfather's tools. Shigeru loved creating. He thought he might want to be a puppeteer or a painter. In high school, he became a fan of manga, a Japanese style of comic book.

OFF TO COLLEGE

In 1970, Miyamoto enrolled at the Kanazawa College of Art in Kanazawa, Japan. Miyamoto knew he wanted to paint, draw, and build things with his hands. He still loved art and storytelling. He spent most of his time drawing, playing early video games, and listening to music.

Miyamoto graduated with a degree in **industrial arts and crafts**. Right away, he put together a **portfolio** filled with samples of the artwork he had created in college. He finally knew what he wanted to do: he wanted to work with toys. Miyamoto gathered his manga and other illustrations he had drawn. He added colorful hand-carved clothes hangers for kids that he had designed. The hangers were shaped like elephants, chickens, and birds. He also added designs for a fun amusement park clock and a seesaw made to hold three kids at once. Once his portfolio was finished, Miyamoto started looking for jobs.

01150   007650

=5   P=01

Radar Scope was one of the first Nintendo games that Miyamoto helped design.

DAMAGE METER

Miyamoto impressed Nintendo president Hiroshi Yamauchi with his playful approach to gaming.

A JOB AT
NINTENDO

After college, Miyamoto was able to get a meeting with Hiroshi Yamauchi, the head of a Japanese game and toy company called Nintendo. Nintendo started as a playing card company in 1889. By the mid-1970s, the company had started

making **arcade** games. Miyamoto thought Nintendo might be the perfect place for him to work.

At first, Yamauchi wasn't interested in hiring Miyamoto. He thought Nintendo needed engineers more than artists, but he agreed to a meeting. Twenty-four-year-old Miyamoto had long, shaggy hair, but he dressed nicely and had good manners. Yamauchi could tell that Miyamoto had a fun, childlike way of looking at the world. This was exactly the kind of creative spark Nintendo needed. Yamauchi invited Miyamoto to come back with samples of his work.

NINTENDO

Japanese artist Fusajiro Yamauchi started Nintendo in 1889 as way to sell his hand-drawn playing cards. In the mid-1960s, the company began dreaming up ideas for toys, including toys called Ultra Hand, the Love Tester, and the Beam Gun. In the 1970s, Nintendo began developing video games for arcades. The company released home gaming systems in Japan and the United States in the mid-1980s. Miyamoto was hired by Hiroshi Yamauchi, the great-grandson of Nintendo's founder.

Miyamoto returned with his portfolio. Yamauchi liked
what he saw. He hired Miyamoto to be the first artist on
Nintendo's staff.

THE WORLD OF NINTENDO

When Miyamoto began his job at Nintendo in 1977, he

THE FIRST VIDEO GAMES

The first video games were available by the early 1970s. *Pong*, one of the first popular video games, appeared in arcades in 1972. It was based on the real game of Ping-Pong, with a single dot representing the ball, a dotted line as the net, and two short lines for paddles. Players moved the paddles to try to hit the ball.

worked in the planning department as an assistant. Miyamoto worked on a variety of projects, including painting panels for arcade machines. One of his first design jobs was to help create Nintendo's *Sheriff* and *Radar Scope* games, both made for arcades. *Radar Scope*, a game in which players shoot attacking spacecraft, was popular in Japan. Nintendo had planned to release the game in the United States, but players lost interest. Nintendo was stuck with several arcade cabinets designed to hold *Radar Scope* games. Yamauchi needed someone to design a new video game to fit into the extra arcade cabinets right away.

The *Donkey Kong* arcade console

Miyamoto accepted the challenge. He liked video games, but he didn't think the Ping-Pong and shooting games popular at the time were very interesting. He also didn't understand why players always had to compete against one another. Miyamoto wanted to design a new kind of game with characters and a story. He thought video games would be much more fun if they were like movies, with players controlling characters in the story and working together toward the same goal.

TECH TALK

"I thought, 'Why [do video games] have to be a competition? Why can't everyone just move together in the same direction, carrying things as a team? Who made these rules in the first place, anyway?'"

—*Shigeru Miyamoto*

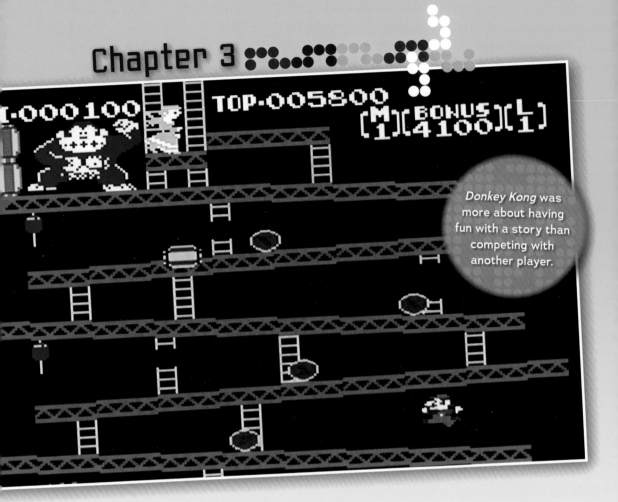

Chapter 3

Donkey Kong was more about having fun with a story than competing with another player.

A NEW KIND OF VIDEO GAME

Under the guidance of Nintendo **game developer** Gunpei Yokoi, Miyamoto went to work designing a video game. Miyamoto's original idea was to create a game based on the story of Popeye, a cartoon sailor. But Nintendo wasn't able to legally use the Popeye characters. So Miyamoto created his own characters.

The game, called *Donkey Kong*, featured a hero character named Mario. Mario was a carpenter who wore a red hat and had a big nose. These features made Mario easy to see on a small screen. The object of the game is for Mario to rescue his girlfriend, Pauline, from his pet ape, Donkey Kong. As Mario moves up ladders and across floors to reach Pauline, Donkey Kong rolls barrels down from the top to knock down Mario. Players must make Mario jump the barrels to continue playing the game.

Nintendo released updates to the popular *Donkey Kong*, including *Donkey Kong 3* in 1983.

Donkey Kong was different from all other games at the time. *Donkey Kong* was not only one of the first games to use a story line, but also it was one of the first platform games. In a platform game, characters walk, run, or jump over objects to reach the next level of the game.

WORKING WITH PROGRAMMERS

Miyamoto was not a **computer programmer**, but he knew what he wanted the characters to do on the screen. He came up with the ideas and checked with his team of programmers to see if they could bring the ideas to life. Miyamoto also worked with engineers to make easy-to-use hand controls for the games.

All of Miyamoto's hard work paid off. *Donkey Kong* was a hit in Japan. But Nintendo employees in the United States were not impressed. They thought the game looked childish and silly. They were convinced that video game fans wanted fast-paced, competitive games that required shooting. But when Nintendo released the game in the United States, the employees were proven wrong. *Donkey Kong* was instantly popular. Nintendo asked Miyamoto to design a follow-up game.

Mario Bros. used popular characters from *Donkey Kong* in a new setting with new challenges.

©1983 Nintendo of Ameri.

MARIO LIVES ON

In 1983, Nintendo released Miyamoto's next game, *Mario Bros.* In it, he moved the action of the original *Donkey Kong* game underground, to the sewer system of New York City. Mario became a plumber and teamed up with his tall brother, Luigi. The game features a set of platforms that players must climb through to save a princess and win the game. Just like *Donkey Kong*, the game was a hit.

That same year, Nintendo released its first home gaming system, called Famicom, in Japan. In 1985, Nintendo released the same system in the United States under a new name: the Nintendo Entertainment System. It quickly outsold all other video game systems. Nintendo released another Mario game, *Super Mario Bros.*, to go with the gaming system. *Super Mario Bros.* became the best-selling video game of its time.

THE LEGEND OF ZELDA

While Miyamoto continued to design the Mario games, he also began working on a completely new game. Just like

With home gaming consoles, Nintendo games went from the arcade to the living room.

MIND MAPPING A GAME

When Miyamoto designs a game, he draws a map of the entire game as it appears on the screen. Then he spreads the drawing out on several tables. He spends several days working his way through the game in his mind. He asks himself questions at every turn. For example, he might ask, "Was this part of the maze fun or frustrating?" If it was frustrating, he adds some type of reward to keep players interested.

Donkey Kong, this new game was among the first of its kind. Released in 1986, *The Legend of Zelda* was one of a new kind of game called action-adventure games. In this type of game, players have more freedom to lead a character through solving a problem. To create the game, Miyamoto pulled ideas from his memories of exploring the woods, hills, and caves around his home in Sonobe. In *The Legend of Zelda*, players guide the main character, Link, on a journey through many different worlds that make up the imaginary land of Hyrule.

Chapter 4

F-ZERO™

GRAND PRIX

In games like *F-Zero Grand Prix*, players didn't directly compete with one another, but they could try to beat high scores from other players around the world.

A WHOLE NEW DIMENSION

During the 1990s, Miyamoto kept working on new Mario games. He and his team also dreamed up new ideas for games, including *F-Zero*, *Wave Race*, and *Star Fox*. Then, in June 1996, Nintendo released Nintendo 64, entering the world of 3-D gaming systems. This meant that characters on the screen appeared in three-dimensional forms, making the games more realistic. Nintendo released *Super Mario 64* with the new system. A 3-D version of *The Legend of Zelda* called *Ocarina of Time* followed in 1998.

Mario Kart 64 continued the adventures of popular characters that first appeared in *Donkey Kong.*

The Nintendo 64 console and controller

Shortly after the Nintendo 64 became available, Miyamoto became a creative director at Nintendo. He led a team that came up with ideas and wrote a story. Then Miyamoto and his team worked with programmers, engineers, and artists to bring the game to life.

ROOTED IN REALITY

In Miyamoto's recent games, the settings have become more realistic. But one thing hasn't changed. Just as *The Legend of Zelda* was based on Miyamoto's childhood adventures, almost all of his new games are based on his own experiences. After Miyamoto and his family got a Shetland sheepdog, he developed *Nintendogs*, a game where players create their own pet and take care of it. In 2001, Miyamoto was inspired to create *Pikmin* after watching ants carry a leaf across his patio. The game follows the adventures of small antlike critters that live in pods called Onions.

PIKMIN MOVIES

In 2014, Miyamoto tried something new. He made a series of Pikmin animated movies based on the adventures of characters in Nintendo's *Pikmin* games. The short films can be viewed online, and viewers can create their own sounds to go along with the movies.

INTRODUCING THE Wii

In 2006, Nintendo released another new gaming system: the Wii. Miyamoto helped create many of the Wii's games. He also helped design the handheld controls. The Wii is able to sense a player's movement and then uses the movement to make the player part of the game.

One of the most popular Wii games has been *Wii Fit*. In this game, players can do yoga, strength training, or track their weight and fitness. Again, Miyamoto pulled from his own experiences to create the game. After turning forty, he began swimming to get into shape. He recorded his weight every day

Miyamoto and Nintendo hoped the Wii system would reach people who would not otherwise play video games.

By 2013, Nintendo had sold more than one hundred million Wii consoles.

on charts he posted at home. His wife and daughter thought his charts were interesting and began to follow along. This gave Miyamoto, who was always trying to find a way to get his wife to play video games, the idea for *Wii Fit*. If easy-to-play video games could be considered a form of exercise, would more people play them? Miyamoto guessed they would, and he was right. Since then, the Wii has transformed video gaming into a social, family activity.

WHAT'S NEXT?

Thanks to Miyamoto's creative ideas, Nintendo has become one of the most successful video game companies in the world. In 2015, Miyamoto worked on Project Giant Robot, a game that allows players to build and operate their own virtual robots. Miyamoto has talked of retiring or slowing down a bit, to allow others to do more developing. But he still has many ideas for new games. Nintendo fans can't wait to see what he comes up with next.

Miyamoto plays *Super Mario World* on Nintendo's Super NES.

TIMELINE

1952

Shigeru Miyamoto is born in Sonobe, Japan, on November 16.

1977

After graduating from the Kanazawa College of Art, Miyamoto is hired by Nintendo as the first artist on staff.

1981

Miyamoto designs one of the first video games to use a story line.

1983

Nintendo releases *Mario Bros.*

1985

Nintendo releases the Nintendo Entertainment System in the United States, where it becomes the best-selling console of its era.

1986

Nintendo releases Miyamoto's *The Legend of Zelda*

1998

Nintendo releases *The Legend of Zelda: Ocarina of Time*. Miyamoto is promoted to creative director at Nintendo.

2006

Nintendo launches the Wii, which Miyamoto helped develop.

2015

Miyamoto works on *Project Giant Robot*, a game that allows players to build and operate their own virtual robots.

SOURCE NOTES

6 Mike Snider, "Q&A: 'Mario' Creator Shigeru Miyamoto," *USA Today*, November 8, 2010, http://content.usatoday.com/communities/gamehunters /post/2010/11/qa-mario-creator-shigeru-miyamoto/1#.VS1ciJTF-QM.

15 Robbie Collin, "Nintendo's Shigeru Miyamoto: 'What Can Games Learn from Film? Nothing,'" *Telegraph* (London), November 10, 2014, http://www .telegraph.co.uk/culture/film/film-news/11201171/nintendo-super-mario -pikmin-tokyo-film-festival-mandarin-oriental-tokyo-sega-mario-kart-zelda-wii -oculus-rift.html.

GLOSSARY

arcade
a building or room filled with different video games, many of them coin- or token-operated

computer programmer
a person who writes the instructions that a computer follows

engineers
people who study how things work and figure out ways to improve the way things work

game developer
a person who creates video games or plays a role in their design and programming

industrial arts and crafts
an area of study that includes making furniture, toys, or other items from wood and drawing

portfolio
an artist's collection of work, including drawings, plans, books, or other completed projects

FURTHER INFORMATION

BOOKS

deWinter, Jennifer. *Shigeru Miyamoto: Super Mario Bros., Donkey Kong, The Legend of Zelda.* New York: Bloomsbury Academic, 2015. Find out more about Shigeru Miyamoto and the famous games he created.

Firestone, Mary. *Nintendo: The Company and Its Founders.* Edina, MN: Abdo, 2011. Read about the history of Nintendo and the people who helped create the company.

Kaplan, Arie. *The Crazy Careers of Video Game Designers.* Minneapolis: Lerner Publications, 2014. Learn about the different roles people play in designing video games.

WEBSITES

Nintendo
https://www.nintendo.com
Explore Nintendo's latest video games and consoles.

Pikmin Short Movies
http://pikmin.nintendo.com
Watch clips from Miyamoto's three short Pikmin movies: *The Night Juicer, Treasure in a Bottle,* and *Occupational Hazards.*

"Shigeru Miyamoto Interview (Creator of Mario!)"
https://www.youtube.com/watch?v=dUkU6O4p7Lw
Learn more about the famous designer from the man himself. Watch this interview with Shigeru Miyamoto.

LERNER

SOURCE

Expand learning beyond the printed book. Download free, complementary educational resources for this book from our website, www.lerneresource.com.

INDEX

ABOUT THE AUTHOR

Kari Cornell is a freelance writer and editor who lives with her husband, two sons, and dog in Minneapolis, Minnesota. One of her favorite things to do is to write about people who've found a way to do what they love. When she's not writing, she likes tinkering in the garden, cooking, and making something clever out of nothing. Learn more about her work at karicornell.wordpress.com.